D0581781

PICTURING SCOTLAND

THE BORDERS

2   The Royal Border Bridge carries the East Coast main line from London to Edinburgh across the River Tweed at Berwick. Opened in 1850, its 28 arches reach a height of 38m/125ft.

THE BORDERS

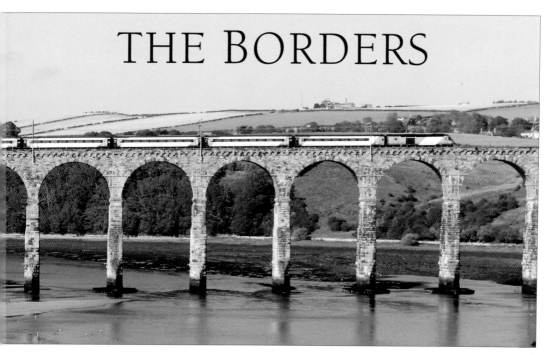

Welcome to the Borders!

The glory of Scotland is the uncanny way its regions and counties are so diverse yet all are distinctively Scottish. So it is with the Borders: you know you are in Scotland and you know there is nowhere else in Scotland you can be. The modern-day region of Scottish Borders comprises the former counties of Berwickshire, Roxburghshire, Selkirkshire and Peeblesshire plus the southern part of Midlothian, yet these earlier entities have merged into a harmonious blend of scenery and settlement. That harmony is due in no small part to the dominance of the River Tweed and its tributaries such as the Teviot and Yarrow. As well as its defining role *within* the region, the Tweed also forms the actual and natural border between England and Scotland from Carham to Berwick.

Mention of Berwick leads to a word of explanation, for this book begins its journey through the Borders at this historically vital town, despite it being 'English' since 1482. Taken from Northumbria by the Scots in 1018, it was granted Royal Burgh status by King David I around 1124. This helped Berwick to grow into one of Scotland's wealthiest trading ports by the late 1200s. For the next 200 years its prosperity declined due to the repeated ravages brought upon it by the conflicts between Scotland and England. Worst of these was the genocide inflicted by Edward I in 1296 when at least 7,500 out of a population of 13,000 were massacred, making this one of the worst atrocities in the history of medieval Britain.

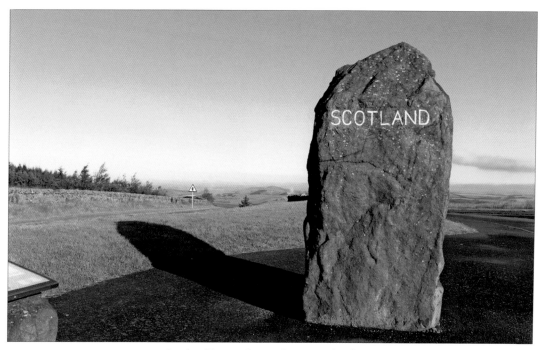

Scotland begins here! This sign of welcome is at Carter Bar where the 5
A68 breasts the summit between England and Scotland.

During its strife-torn centuries it changed hands, on average, once every 15 years. As a result of its frontier status, it became one of the most fortified towns in Britain, leaving a legacy that is a major reason to visit the town today. Beginning at Berwick is a good way to make sense of the region's story.

An exploration of the Borders is a journey through Scotland's history. As part of the frontier with England, incursions, cattle-raiding, skirmishes and full-blown battles formed a centuries-long backdrop to daily life. Towerhouse castles like Neidpath near Peebles speak of this era. Later, when the thirst for strife declined, some of these castles evolved into more palatial dwellings, as demonstrated by Thirlestane Castle just outside Lauder. From the Georgian era to Edwardian times, country mansions like Mellerstain and Manderston appeared. The four great Border Abbeys of Dryburgh, Jedburgh, Kelso and Melrose, founded by King David I, survived their share of the region's troubles for centuries, only to be brought to final ruin by Henry VIII of England's

A view of Dryburgh Abbey. See also p.81.

'Rough Wooing' in the 16th century. The fertility of the land in the valleys is evident both in terms of arable and livestock farms. The textiles industry gave rise to towns like Hawick and Galashiels, still home to leading brands even if much of the manufacturing is done elsewhere.

So this book begins its journey in Berwick and embarks on a broadly circular tour of the region, during the course of which it aims to present the huge range of sites and scenery that give the Borders their special charm. Travelling in a clockwise direction means we begin by tracing the border with England as far as the Cheviot Hills, where the Pennine Way terminates at Kirk Yetholm. After dipping south towards the border with Dumfries and Galloway, we turn north through the hillscapes between numerous dales, coming within sight of Lanarkshire before turning west to zigzag our way back across to the North Sea coast. Whether your interests lie in architecture and townscapes or landscapes and rural rides, the Borders deliver a host of images that combine to make a most memorable tour.

The town of Duns, where the medieval theologian and philosopher John Duns Scotus was born c.1265.

8 The inviting panorama of the Borders from Carter Bar. This northerly view gives an idea of the terrain and scenery that waits to be explored. In 1575 Carter Bar was the scene of the Raid of the Redeswire.

This was the last major battle between the Kingdom of England and the Kingdom of Scotland.

10 This picture makes it clear that Berwick-upon-Tweed is an important bridging point! The Old Bridge in the foreground was built from 1611 to 1624. The middle, larger-span road bridge dates to 1928.

Berwick's town walls provide some good viewpoints from which to appreciate the town centre. **11**
Where the wall crosses Castlegate, this view looks down Marygate to the Town Hall.

12 Huge bastions still surround Berwick on all sides except the south, where the River Tweed provides a natural defence. This is part of the northern ramparts, with cannon still in place.

Given Berwick's location it's no surprise that it is garrisoned: Ravensdowne Barracks are Britain's oldest, **13** begun in 1717. Inset: the crest of the King's Own Scottish Borderers, based here from 1881 to 1964.

14 A few miles west of Berwick, on the banks of the river Tweed, is Paxton House. Built by the Adam brothers in 1758, it is perhaps the finest example of 18th century Palladian Country houses in Britain.

Summer serenity on the River Tweed at Paxton. Two of the estate's fishing boats are drawn up on the bank. From its source at Tweed's Well the river flows for 156km/97 miles through the Borders. **15**

16 Continuing westwards, the village of Coldstream is situated at the lowest fording point on the Tweed. This is Henderson Park, with the Coldstream Guards Stone in the foreground.

Coldstream Museum's Guards Gallery, pictured here, tells the story of the Coldstream Guards. The **17** origins of the regiment go back to 1650, when it was formed at the instruction of Oliver Cromwell.

18 Southwards now, and the sun has just risen over the Cheviot Hills and begins to illuminate the slopes surrounding the villages of Town and Kirk Yetholm. The latter (pictured) is at the end of the Pennine Way.

The attractive village of Town Yetholm in autumn. The name Yetholm means the 'place at the gate', **19** from the old Scots 'yett' meaning a gate and 'holm' or 'ham', the Anglo-Saxon for a settlement.

20 Travelling north-west from Yetholm we reach the impressive town of Kelso. The town centre is charming, with its fine architecture, floral displays and cobbled streets, as in this view down Horsemarket.

Kelso boasts the largest market square in Scotland, the scale of which can be appreciated in this **21** picture. The grandest building on the square is the Cross Keys Hotel, built in 1760 as a coaching inn.

22 More floral flair at the War Memorial gardens, just along Bridge Street from the square. Viewed from the other end (see opposite), they provide a lovely foreground to the remains of Kelso Abbey.

Little remains of Kelso Abbey today, yet the stature of what still stands gives a clear clue to its former **23** grandeur. Built with two crossings and two towers, its layout was also unique in Scotland.

24 Floors Castle is built on a natural terrace overlooking the River Tweed, facing the Cheviot Hills, and is the home of the Roxburghe Family. It is based on a tower house which was added to by William Adam

from 1721. William Playfair then remodelled the castle between 1837 and 1847. The result is a romantic **25** fairytale castle with its roofscape of turrets, pinnacles and cupolas, which this picture seeks to emphasise.

26 The Walled Garden at Floors Castle is a wonderful treat for anyone who enjoys the delights of spectacular herbaceous borders and expertly tended shrubs and plants of all types.

South of Kelso, the shapes of the fields, the texture of their cultivation and the folds in the land itself **27** form this 'patchwork quilt' agricultural landscape. These fields are near the village of Eckford.

28 Laburnum tunnel at Monteviot House Gardens. Extending to some 30 acres, the gardens include a formal rose garden, herb garden, herbaceous perennial river garden and an Oriental-style water garden.

Continuing south into Jedburgh, first stop is the Castle Jail, a 19th-century Howard Reform prison **29** built on the site of a 12th-century castle. Today it is a museum that recreates prison life in the 1800s.

30 Jedburgh is the most intact of the 'big four' abbeys, with its virtually complete nave, tower and north transept. This is astonishing given the number of times it was attacked during the Anglo-Scottish wars.

Left: visitors enjoy the peaceful atmosphere of the abbey. Right: Jedburgh's Mercat Cross **31** is a work of art that makes a striking centrepiece at the heart of the town.

32 Looking at the immaculate state of Jedburgh's Market Place today, it is hard to imagine what life was like in the strife-torn Middle Ages. It suffered attack or occupation 11 times from 1296 to 1548.

This is the house where Mary, Queen of Scots, stayed during a visit to Jedburgh in 1566. Today the **33** house contains a unique collection of objects and pictures that give an insight into her tragic life.

34 Our most southerly point is Hermitage Castle, which stands in lonely isolation about five miles north of Newcastleton. This dark picture reflects its reputation as 'guardhouse of the bloodiest valley in Britain'.

As this aerial picture shows, Hawick is a substantial town, the largest in the Borders, with a population **35** of just under 18,000. Its growth was based on the textiles industry, which remains important.

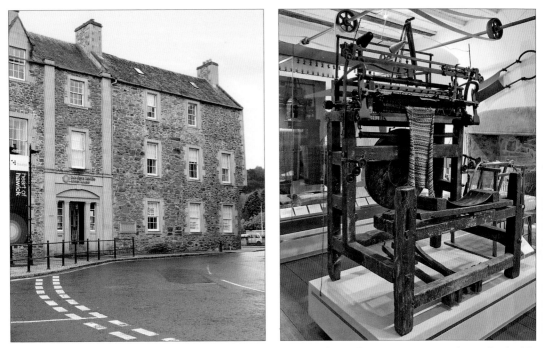

36 Left: In the centre of Hawick, the 16th-century Black Tower of Drumlanrig is incorporated into this building, which houses the Borders Textile Towerhouse Museum. Right: Hand Stocking Frame in the museum.

Left: Angela Hunter's statue depicts William of Rule 'turning' an angry bull to save the life of Robert the Bruce. The surname 'Turnbull' originates from this incident. Right: a heron on Slitrig Water, Hawick. **37**

38 This is the Walter Elliot Room in Hawick Museum. Once a civil servant in India, naturalist Sir Walter Elliot returned to his ancestral home near Hawick in the 1870s. This exhibit recreates his study.

Leaving Hawick behind we now head for the 'wild west' of the Borders. This scene, from a viewpoint above the village of Roberton, looks to the south and captures a hill farm on a day of changing light. 39

40 The road through Roberton goes over the hills that divide Teviotdale from Ettrickdale. This view, a few miles south-west of Ettrickbridge, exemplifies Borders scenery as the land rises towards the hills

that line the western edge of the region. The poet and novelist James Hogg ('The Ettrick Shepherd', **41** 1770-1835) hailed from this dale and is buried in the churchyard at Ettrick, a few miles further on.

42 A long-abandoned farm building in Ettrickdale shows nature reclaiming the land for itself. As the tree grows, it is steadily demolishing the stonework.

Traversing another ridge of hills we head north into the next dale, where the Yarrow Water, **43** seen here near the Gordon Arms, flows for 13 miles from St Mary's Loch to the Tweed.

44 From the hamlet of Cappercleuch by St Mary's Loch, the first snow of winter is seen on the slopes of the hills between here and Tweeddale, which rise above the Megget Reservoir.

And so to St Mary's Loch itself, the largest natural loch in the Borders at just over five kms/three miles **45** long. It takes its name from a church dedicated to St Mary that once stood on the northern shore.

46 Immediately south of St Mary's Loch is the smaller but equally lovely Loch of the Lowes, seen here on an autumn evening.

The minor road west from Cappercleuch to Tweedsmuir takes in some dramatic scenery, especially where **47**
it passes Talla Linn falls. A series of cascades, like this one, sees the burn drop hundreds of feet in total.

48 The burn feeds Talla Reservoir, pictured here from near the top of the falls on a windy day that produced rapidly changing patterns of light and shade.

On a calmer day, morning light begins to illuminate the countryside between Broughton and Biggar. **49**
This is the western limit of the Borders – Biggar, just a few miles on, is in South Lanarkshire.

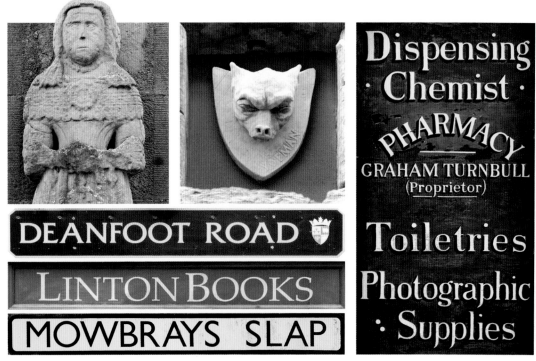

50 A northerly hop takes us to West Linton, where this array of signs and architectural detail are indicative of a village full of life and points of interest. The carved creature can be found on the Manor House.

Not far from Peebles, Dawyck Botanic Garden offers many horticultural treats, including carpets of snow- **51**
drops in February. Since 1979 Dawyck has been in the care of the Royal Botanic Garden Edinburgh.

52 En route from Dawyck to Peebles, Neidpath Castle can be seen in its commanding position on the banks of the Tweed. The L-plan castle dates back to the 14th century.

Peebles benefits from an idyllic setting and has been developed in a manner which makes the **53** most of its natural gifts, as this picture of the parkland by the Tweed demonstrates.

54 Even a winter night in Peebles can make for a striking image, with the floodlit Old Parish Church standing tall above the fast-flowing river.

Left: this stained glass window in the Old Parish Church beautifully illustrates local scenes.   **55**
Right: Cross Kirk tower, the centrepiece of the ruins of a church complex begun in the late 1100s.

56 Peebles is surrounded by hills that offer a number of great walks. For example, the 15-mile Dun Rig Horseshoe takes in the four peaks surrounding Glensax with extensive views like this one in all directions.

58 Peebles is a busy town with a High Street full of characterful architecture. Among many points of interest are the Tweeddale Museum and Gallery and the unusually elaborate War Memorial.

Heading east from Peebles, our next destination is Innerleithen. Pictured just north of the town, this is Leithen Water, the source of which rises in the Moorfoot Hills.

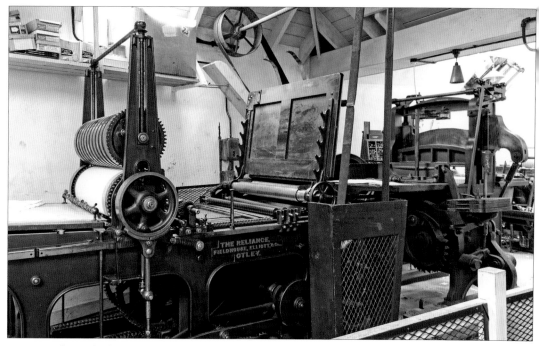

60 One of Innerleithen's attractions is the preserved Robert Smail's Printing Works. Visitors can see the printing presses in action and try their hand at traditional typesetting.

Also not to be missed in Innerleithen is St Ronan's Well Visitor Centre. This historic spa hosts exhibitions telling the story of the town and St Ronan's Well.

62 Just to the south of Innerleithen is the wonderful Traquair House which has the distinction of being Scotland's oldest inhabited residence. Dating back to 1107, it was originally a royal hunting lodge.

An excellent way to continue from Traquair is along the Southern Upland Way long distance walk, **63** which goes over the hills via the Three Brethren boundary cairns, built in the 1500s.

64 South of the Three Brethren, in the valley of Yarrow Water, stands Bowhill. This house of unique grandeur is the Scottish Borders home of the Duke of Buccleuch KBE.

Aikwood Tower overlooks Ettrick Water. From 1517 the site belonged to the Scotts of Aikwood, **65** who built the tower during the 1540s. Today it is a desirable venue for functions and weddings.

66 Moving on to Selkirk, this is Halliwell House Museum. It recreates the building's former use as a home and an ironmonger's shop and also tells the story of the historic burgh of Selkirk.

The Halliwell name remains active in present-day retailing, as this award-winning butcher's shop in **67** Selkirk shows. It also typifies how Borders towns retain a high proportion of independent shops.

68 Sir Walter Scott is the greatest literary figure associated with the Borders. He designed and built his magnificent home, Abbotsford, overlooking the Tweed just outside Galashiels.

The entrance hall at Abbotsford. Visitors can also see Sir Walter's study, **69** drawing room, armoury and dining room.

70 Galashiels is another textile town that has diversified in more recent times. Cornmill Fountain makes use of the old lade from a demolished corn mill and forms this water feature in front of the Burgh Chambers.

Bank Street Gardens provide a pleasant place to relax. Galashiels is built on the banks of **71** Gala Water about a mile from its confluence with the Tweed.

72 The Borders are famous for the 'Common Ridings', the centrepiece of each one being a ceremonial rideout around local boundaries. This is the Galashiels event, known as the Braw Lads' Day.

Another short hop east brings us to the lovely town of Melrose, set at the foot of the Eildon Hills **73** (see front cover). This is the Market Place with the Mercat Cross on the right.

74 Melrose Abbey is a magnificent ruin on a grand scale. It was founded in 1136 by Cistercian monks at the request of King David I. It is also the burial place of Robert the Bruce's heart.

The anatomy of the Abbey church: its ruined state allows inspection of internal and external 75 features simultaneously. Despite the devastation, much delicate stonework remains.

76 To the north of the church there are extensive remnants that show the layout of other parts of the abbey. These are the footings of the lay brothers range with the Commendator's (Abbot's) House on the right.

Beside the Abbey is Priorwood Garden with its herbaceous borders, orchard and dried flower garden. 77
The nearby Harmony Garden is also worth a visit while in Melrose.

78 Now a little detour to the north is required to take in the small town of Lauder where the Old Parish Church is unique. It is the only cruciform church with an octagonal central tower in Scotland.

On the eastern edge of Lauder is Thirlestane Castle. It is a first-class example of how what began as a fort in the 13th century has evolved into a stately home of immense proportions and unique appearance.

80 Heading south again via a back road on the eastern side of the valley near Melrose opens up this view of Leaderfoot viaduct, a monument to the long-abandoned railway network that used to serve the Borders.

Dryburgh Abbey (see also p.6) is the last of the 'big four' Borders Abbeys on this tour. Its rural location **81** gives it a very different atmosphere from the urban settings of the other three. Peace reigns here.

82 Not far from Dryburgh is the extensive village of St Boswells. The Green, seen here, is said to be the largest village green in Scotland. The village's name derives from St Boisil, an abbot of Melrose.

Smailholm Tower is a remarkably well-preserved fortified home built in the first half of the 15th century. It stands on a prominent ridge-top location a few miles east of St Boswells.

84 Rome wasn't built in a day and the same can certainly be said of Mellerstain. Begun in 1725 and completed in 1778, this grand stately home has a fascinating history and is of unique architectural interest.

Privately owned but available for functions, historic 14th-century Duns Castle is situated in the **85** rolling hills, fields and forests of the Borders on the edge of the little market town of Duns.

86 The home of Lord Palmer, Manderston is the Edwardian House *par excellence*. It was built with no expense spared and with every modern convenience of that era. It can be found just east of Duns.

We now return to the Borders coast where the port of Eyemouth is full of interest such as the fort on **87** the right, to the left of which is Gunsgreen House where visitors can discover the secrets of smuggling.

88 Spectacular coastal scenery around the village of St Abbs. Although the village was only developed from 1833, its name is derived from a Northumbrian princess of long ago: Aebbe founded a

monastery c.635 on the coast just north of here, hence this has become known as St Abbs Head and the village took the same name. Today this area is a National Nature Reserve.

90 Long ago, smuggling was big business in these parts. Eyemouth Maritime Centre, pictured here, has a feature on smuggling as part of its remit of telling the story of mankind afloat.

Eyemouth remains a busy fishing port – this boat is about to land its catch. The harbour is home to **91** a wide range of vessels and has an active boat repair yard, so a walk around it is always rewarding.

92 The pretty village of Coldingham is just north of Eyemouth. Coldingham Priory is the still-impressive remnant of a much larger complex that was founded c.1098 at the request of King Edgar.

The rugged terrain of St Abbs Head is an ideal nesting place for seabirds; in summer tens of thousands **93** of them inhabit the cliffs and stacks on which they are relatively safe from predators.

94 St. Abbs Head Lighthouse is one of the principal lights in Scotland and marks the southern entrance to the Firth of Forth. Inset: Sea Thrift grows abundantly here.

The bay by the northern tip of St Abbs Head is known as Pettico Wick. From here we look north towards the Lothians – but that's another journey and another book . . .

Published 2012 by Ness Publishing, 47 Academy Street, Elgin, Moray, IV30 1LR
Phone 01343 549663   www.nesspublishing.co.uk

All photographs © Colin Nutt except p.14 © The Paxton Trust; p.28 © Monteviot House; p.35 © Guthrie Aerial Photography; pp.56/57 & 63 © Keith Fergus; p.64 © Bowhill Country Estate; p.69 © Eric Wright; p.72 © Grant Kinghorn; p.85 © Duns Castle

Text © Colin Nutt
ISBN 978-1-906549-19-0

All rights reserved. No part of this publication may be reproduced, stored in a retrieval system, in any form or by any means, without prior permission of Ness Publishing. The right of Colin Nutt as author of this work has been asserted by him in accordance with the Copyright, Designs and Patents Act 1988.

Front cover: Scott's View, north of St Boswells; p.1: fishing boat off St Abbs Head; p.4: at the Curiosity Shop in Jedburgh; this page: rainbow over St Abbs church; back cover: afterglow over the Tweed at Innerleithen.

For a list of websites and phone numbers please turn over >

Websites and phone numbers (where available) for principal places featured in this book in order of appearance:

The Borders: www.scotborders.org.uk
Berwick-upon-Tweed: www.exploreberwick.co.uk
Dryburgh Abbey: www.historic-scotland.gov.uk (T) 01835 822381
Paxton House: www.paxtonhouse.co.uk (T) 01289 386291
Coldstream: www.coldstream-scotland.co.uk
Coldstream Museum: www.scotborders.gov.uk/outabout/visit/museums (T) 01890 882630
Yetholm: www.yetholmonline.org.uk
Kelso: www.kelso.bordernet.co.uk
Kelso Abbey: www.historic-scotland.gov.uk (T) 01896 822562
Floors Castle: www.roxburghe.net/floors_castle (T) 01573 223333
Monteviot: www.monteviot.com (T) 01835 830380
Jedburgh: www.jedburgh.org.uk .
Jedburgh Abbey: www.historic-scotland.gov.uk (T) 01835 863925
Hermitage Castle: www.historic-scotland.gov.uk (T) 01387 376222
Hawick: www.hawick.net
Borders Textiles Towerhouse: www.heartofhawick.co.uk/drumlanrig (T) 01450 377615
Hawick Museum: www.museumsgalleriesscotland.org.uk/.../hawick-museum-gallery (T) 01450 373457
West Linton: http://www.west-linton.org.uk/
Dawyck Botanic Garden: www.rbge.org.uk/the-gardens/dawyck (T) 01721 760254
Neidpath Castle: www.neidpathcastle.com (T) 01875 870201
Peebles: www.peebles.info
Cross Kirk: www.historic-scotland.gov.uk
Tweeddale Museum and Gallery: www.museumsgalleriesscotland.org.uk/tweeddale-museum (T) 01721 724820
Robert Smail's Printing Works: www.nts.org.uk (T) 0844 493 2259
St Ronan's Well: www.scotborders.gov.uk/directory/st_ronans_wells_visitor_centre (T) 01896 833583